Car Mania

CONCEPT CARS

Ryan James

A Stingray Book

SEAHORSE PUBLISHING

Teaching Tips for Caregivers and Teachers:

This Hi-Lo book features high-interest subject matter that will appeal to all readers in intermediate and middle school grades. It may be enjoyed by students reading at or above grade level as well as by those who are looking for age-appropriate themes matched with a less challenging reading level. Hi-Lo books are ideal for ELL readers, too.

Each book appeals to a striving reader's age and maturity level. Opportunities are provided for students to read words they already know while encountering a limited number of new, high-interest vocabulary words. With these supports in place, students will read more fluently while increasing reading comprehension. Use the following suggestions to help students grow as readers.

- Encourage the student to read independently at home.
- Encourage the student to practice reading aloud.
- Encourage activities that require reading.
- Establish a regular reading time.
- Have the student write questions about what they read.

Teaching Tips for Teachers:

Before Reading

- Ask, "What do I know about this topic?"
- Ask, "What do I want to learn about this topic?"

During Reading

- Ask, "What is the author trying to teach me?"
- Ask, "How is this like something I already know?"

After Reading

- Discuss how the text features (headings, index, etc.) help with understanding the topic.
- Ask, "What interesting or fun fact did you learn?"

TABLE OF CONTENTS

WHAT IS A CONCEPT CAR?

A concept car is an **experimental** model car.

Car **manufacturers** use them to show cutting-edge technology and new ideas.

Then, they take the things that people like and put them in new cars that they sell.

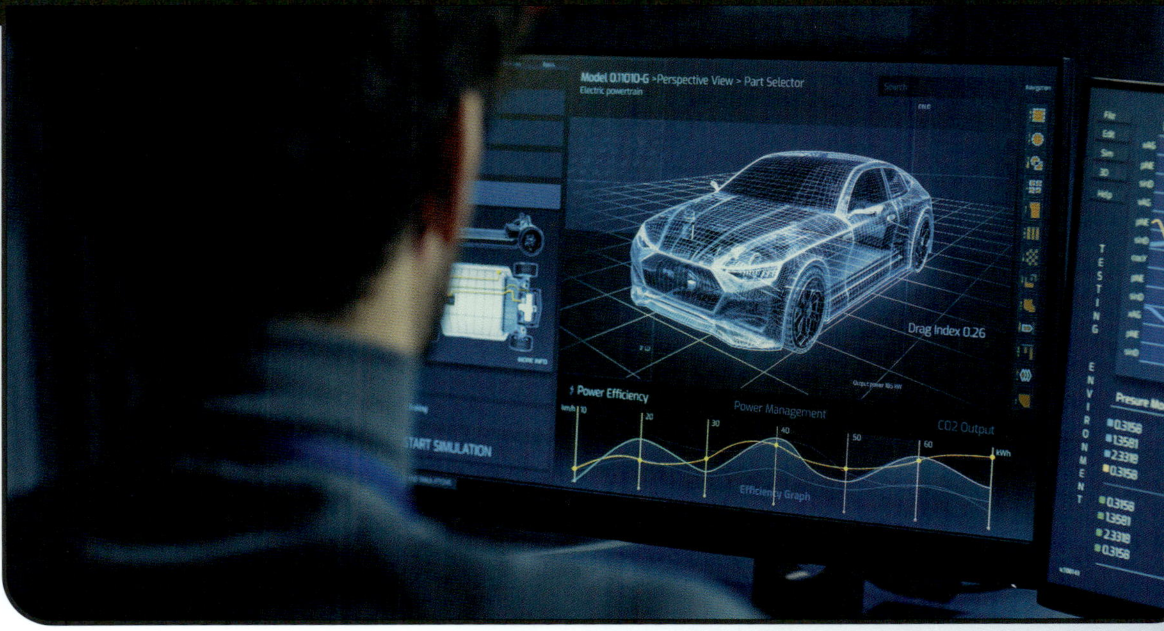
Model 0.11010-G >Perspective View > Part Selector
Electric powertrain
Drag Index 0.26
Power Efficiency
Power Management
CO2 Output
Efficiency Graph
START SIMULATION
TESTING
ENVIRONMENT

THE FIRST CONCEPT CAR

Harley J. Earl was the first person to come up with a concept car.

In 1938, he oversaw the making of the Buick Y-Job while working for General Motors.

It was the first car to have a retractable soft top, wraparound bumpers, and electric windows.

FUN FACTS

Buick still uses the vertical waterfall grille design from the Buick Y-Job.

CONCEPT CARS TAKE FLIGHT

Concept cars in the 1950s were influenced by the Jet Age.

In 1951, Harley J. Earl helped design the LeSabre, which was inspired by a jet fighter plane.

It had hidden headlights and introduced the 12-volt electrical system that is still used in cars today.

CONCEPT CARS CHANGE WITH THE TIMES

In the 1970s, gasoline shortages drove carmakers to design cars that were more fuel-efficient.

Engineers at Mercedes-Benz created a concept car that used less fuel.

In 2007, Chevrolet **debuted** a concept car called the Volt.

It was originally all-electric, but General Motors made it a **hybrid** in the final design to be sold to the public.

FUN FACTS

The Astrolab concept car was created to have zero emissions. It had no roof and relied on solar power to recharge its batteries.

DESIGNING A CONCEPT CAR

Concept cars take years to get created.

First, designers sketch their ideas.

Then, they make clay models called **mock-ups**.

Computer software helps engineers design the cars in detail.

FITTING IN

Car creators try to make concept cars fit with the design of other cars made by the same company.

They might use **chassis** shapes, headlamps, or stripes that have already been successful.

These **design cues** can make a concept car look like a newer version of an older car.

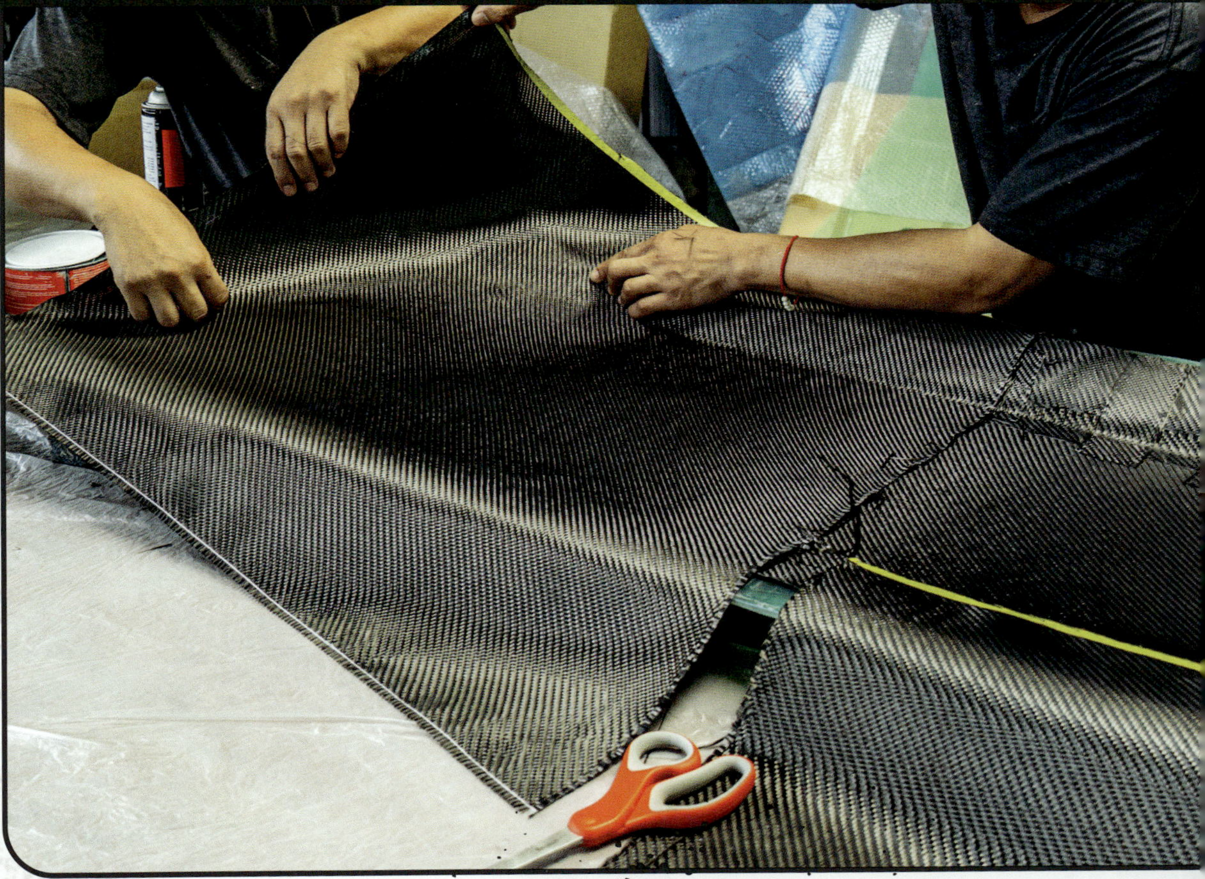

FUN FACTS

Carbon fiber is a common material used for making concept cars.

SHOWING OFF

911 Speedster Concep

Carmakers show off their concept cars at car shows. Concept cars are sometimes called show cars.

Car shows are popular in the United States.

Every year, they are held in large cities such as Los Angeles and Detroit.

SECRETS REVEALED

Manufacturers keep their concept cars a secret until the show.

They want to know what people think about their concept cars and hope they like the new ideas.

Car shows are filled with car **enthusiasts**. They can't wait to find out about the newest ideas in car design.

CONCEPT VS. REALITY

CONCEPT

2005 Lexus LF-A
V-10 engine
500 horsepower
Gasoline-powered

2009 Tesla Model S
AC dual motor
320 horsepower
Electric-powered

1999 Bugatti Veyron EB 18.4
18-cylinder engine
1,000 horsepower
Gasoline-powered

REALITY

2010 Lexus LFA

V-10 engine
552 horsepower
Gasoline-powered

2012 Tesla Model S

AC dual motor
360 horsepower
Electric-powered

2005 Bugatti Veyron

16-cylinder engine
1,000 horsepower
Gasoline-powered

GLOSSARY

chassis (CHAS-ee): the frame of a vehicle on which the body is assembled

debuted (day-BYOOD): made a first public appearance

design cues (di-ZINE kyoos): details in shape, style, or appearance that link things together

enthusiasts (en-THOO-zee-ists): people who are passionate about a particular subject or activity

experimental (ik-sper-uh-MEN-tuhl): not yet thoroughly tested or proven

hybrid (HYE-brid): something made by combining two or more things; hybrid vehicles are powered by both electricity and gas

manufacturers (man-yuh-FAK-chur-uhrs): companies that make products in a factory

mock-ups (MAHK-ups): samples or models built for study, testing, or display

INDEX

AFTER READING QUESTIONS

1. What was the first concept car?
2. What inspired the LeSabre concept car?
3. What helps engineers design the details of concept cars?
4. Name three car features that have appeared on concept cars.
5. What goals do car companies achieve by making concept cars?

ABOUT THE AUTHOR

Ryan James lives in Western North Carolina with his dog Bailey. His favorite race to watch is the Daytona 500. His dream is to own a Lamborghini. When he's not writing books, you can find him backpacking through Pisgah Forest, North Carolina.

Written by: Ryan James
Design by: Kathy Walsh
Editor: Kim Thompson

Library of Congress PCN Data
Concept Cars / Ryan James
Car Mania
ISBN 978-1-63897-471-0 (hard cover)
ISBN 978-1-63897-586-1 (paperback)
ISBN 978-1-63897-701-8 (EPUB)
ISBN 978-1-63897-816-9 (eBook)
Library of Congress Control Number: 2022933099

Printed in the United States of America.

Seahorse Publishing Company
www.seahorsepub.com

Published in the United States
Seahorse Publishing
PO Box 771325
Coral Springs, FL 33077

SEAHORSE PUBLISHING